Great People
of the Bible

15 inductive studies
for neighborhood,
student, and
church groups

Harold Shaw Publishers
Wheaton, Illinois

We gratefully acknowledge the use of these materials that have appeared previously in Harold Shaw publications:

Studies 1, 3, 11, and 12 from Women Who Believed God, © 1983 by Winnie Christensen; Study 6 from Women Who Achieved for God, © 1984 by Winnie Christensen; Study 2 from Genesis: Walking with God, © 1979, 1991 by Margaret Fromer & Sharrel Keyes; Studies 4 and 16 from Relationships, © 1983 by Gladys Hunt; Studies 7 and 10 from Ruth & Daniel: God's People in an Alien Society, © 1986 by Penelope J. Stokes; Study 8 from David: Man After God's Own Heart, Volume II, © 1981 by Robbie Castleman; Study 8 from Elijah: Obedience in a Threatening World, © 1986 by Robbie Castleman; Study 13 from 1 & 2 Peter, Jude: Called for a Purpose, © 1987 by Steve & Dee Brestin; Study 14 from Paul: Thirteenth Apostle (Acts 13–28), © 1986 by Chuck & Winnie Christensen.

Editor: Carol Plueddemann

Cover photo: Dodge Photo

ISBN 0-87788-333-5

99   98   97   96   95   94   93   92

10   9   8   7   6   5   4

CONTENTS

INTRODUCTION

Great people of the Bible—what is the mark of their greatness?

As you go through these studies, you will be struck by the ordinariness of extraordinary lives! These great heroes of the past struggled with difficult family relationships, failure, illness, poverty, death, war, temptation, and loneliness—the same challenges we face today. Sometimes they conquered. Sometimes they failed. Always they experienced God's faithfulness.

God used these ordinary people in significant, sometimes spectacular, ways. He shaped their lives through trials and challenges. Hebrews 11 summarizes the mark of their greatness: ". . . who through *faith* conquered kingdoms, administered justice, and gained what was promised; who shut the mouths of lions, quenched the fury of flames, and escaped the edge of the sword; whose weakness was turned to strength . . ."

These great people can give us encouragement and hope for our lives today. We have the same resource that they had—faith in a great God.

HOW TO USE THIS STUDYGUIDE

Inductive study literally *leads us into* the Bible. By asking questions about its content and searching for answers, we experience the joy of personal discovery. Each group member explores for himself or herself what God is saying. As we read the Bible and discuss the meaning of a passage in our group, we come to certain conclusions about it, and about how we should respond to it. This is quite different from the process in which a teacher *tells* a group *about* the Bible and what it means and what to do about it. In inductive study God speaks directly to each of us through his Word.

A group functions best with a leader keeping the discussion on target, but this leader is neither the teacher nor the answer person. A leader's responsibility is to *ask*, not to *tell*, and to facilitate meaningful discussion by perceptive questions. The answers must come from the text itself as group members examine it, think about it, and talk to each other about it.

Inductive questions are asked at three levels of understanding:
1/What does the text *say?* (Observation)
2/What does the text *mean?* (Interpretation)
3/What does the text *mean to me?* (Personal application)
It is important to get the basic facts first; only after you have digested this factual information can you interpret accurately. And only after you have fully discussed the meaning of a passage will you be able to take the next step and apply the Bible to your daily life.

Fisherman Bible Studyguides provide spaces between questions for jotting down responses, comments, and related questions you would like to raise in the group. Each group member should have a copy of the studyguide, and may take a turn in leading the group.

A group should use any accurate, modern translation of the Bible such as the *New International Version,* the *New American Standard Bible,* the *Revised Standard Version,* the *New Jerusalem Bible,* or the *Good News Bible.* (Other translations or paraphrases of the Bible may be referred to when additional help is needed.) Bible commentaries should not be brought to a Bible study because they tend to dampen discussion and keep people from thinking for themselves.

SUGGESTIONS FOR GROUP LEADERS

Preparing the Study

1/Read and study the Bible passage thoroughly beforehand, grasping its themes and applying its teachings for yourself. First read the passage for content and overview, asking yourself, "Why is this passage important? What principles does it emphasize?" Then, using the studyguide, think through each question and note your findings. Pray that the Holy Spirit will "guide you into truth" so that your leadership will guide others.

2/If the studyguide's questions ever seem ambiguous or unnatural to you, rephrase them in your own words, feeling free to add others that seem necessary to bring out the meaning of a verse.

Leading the study

3/Begin (and end) the study promptly. Start by asking someone to pray for God's help. Remember, He is the teacher, not you!

4/Ask for volunteers to read the passages out loud.

5/As you ask the studyguide's questions in sequence, encourage everyone to participate in the discussion. If some are silent, ask, "What do you think, Betty?" or, "Bill, what can you add to that answer?" or suggest, "Let's have an answer from someone who hasn't spoken up yet."

6/If a question comes up that you can't answer, don't be afraid to admit that you're baffled! Assign the topic as a research project for someone to report on next week.

7/Keep the discussion moving and on target. Though tangents will inevitably be introduced, you can firmly bring the discussion back to the topic at hand. For the group to have a sense of progress and completion, learn to pace the discussion so that you finish a study each session you meet.

8/Don't be afraid of silences: some questions take time to answer and some people need time to gather courage to speak. If silence persists, rephrase your question, but resist the temptation to answer it yourself!

9/If someone comes up with an answer that is clearly illogical or unbiblical, ask gently, "Which verse suggests that idea to you?"

10/Discourage Bible-hopping and over-use of cross-references. Learn all you can from *this* passage, along with the few important references suggested in the studyguide.

11/For further information on getting a new Bible study group started and keeping it functioning effectively, read Gladys Hunt's *You Can Start a Bible Study Group: Making Friends, Changing Lives* and Sharrel Keyes's *Working Out Together: Keeping Your Group in Shape,* available from Harold Shaw Publishers, Box 567, Wheaton, IL 60189.

SUGGESTIONS FOR GROUP MEMBERS

1/Learn and apply the following ground rules for effective inductive Bible study. (If new members join the group later, review these guidelines with the whole group.)

2/Remember that your goal is to learn all that you can *from the Bible passage being studied.* Let it speak for itself without using Bible commentaries or other Bible passages. There is more than enough in each passage assigned in the studyguide to keep your group productively occupied for one session. Sticking to the assigned passage saves the group from insecurity and confusion.

3/Avoid the temptation to bring up those fascinating tangents that don't really grow out of the passage you are discussing. If the topic is of common interest, you can bring it up later in informal conversation following the study. Meanwhile, help each other stick to the passage!

4/Encourage each other to participate. People remember best what they discover and verbalize for themselves. Some people are naturally shyer or more reticent than others, or they may be afraid of making a mistake. If your discussion is free and friendly and you show real interest in what other group members think and feel, they will be more likely to speak up.

Remember, the more people involved in a discussion, the richer it will be. Never condemn or criticize another's opinion. Suggest an alternative view in a spirit of love, if you can back it up from the Bible passage under discussion.

5/Guard yourself from answering too many questions or talking too much. Give others a chance to express themselves. If you are one who participates easily, discipline yourself by counting to ten before you open your mouth!

6/Make personal, honest applications and commit yourself to letting God's Word change you.

ADAM AND EVE

Like Adam and Eve, we know ourselves to rank somewhere between animals and angels. We are dust and also "living souls." We face God as our Source, but we shrink from him as our moral judge. What we remember only occasionally about ourselves stands out boldly in these early chapters of the Bible.

1

ADAM AND EVE

GENESIS 1:26–31; 2:4–7, 15–25; 3:1–24; 4:1–2, 25–26; 5:1–4

Read Genesis 1:26–31.

1/What made Adam and Eve distinctly different from the rest of creation? In what ways do you think men and women reflect the "image of God"?

2/What joint responsibility and privileges did God give that first man and woman? How did God evaluate his special creation?

Read Genesis 2:4–7, 15–25.

3/What additional responsibilities and privileges were given to man in this more detailed account of man's creation? What limits did God set (verse 17)?

4/When God brought Adam and Eve together, what principles did he establish for marriage (verse 24)?

5/What ideals and hopes do you think God had for that first man and woman? How would you describe their relationship to God? To each other? To their environment?

Read Genesis 3:1–24.

6/What insinuation about God did the serpent make to Eve (verses 1, 4–5)? (The serpent is later identified as Satan.)

7/What immediate effect did Eve's choice have on her and her husband? On their relationship with God?

8/What negative and positive predictions about the future did God make to Eve and Adam?

9/What role would the woman play in the fulfillment of God's promise (verse 15)?

Note: The "offspring" of verse 15 is Jesus. Satan would strike his heel, but Jesus would crush Satan's head.

10/How did Adam respond to this message of hope (verse 20)? In light of the nature of God's judgment, what was significant about his responses?

Read Genesis 4:1–2, 25–26; 5:1–4.

11/When Eve named her son Cain, how was she expressing her faith in God's promise of 3:15? Cain proved to be a bitter disappointment to Eve. Abel was the godly son, but Cain murdered him. How did Eve's response to Seth's birth (verse 25) show that her hope was still in God?

12/How can we experience a new beginning when we sin? Read 1 John 1:7, 9; Psalm 103:3,12. In what specific ways can Adam and Eve be examples of challenge and encouragement to us?

For further study on Adam and Eve, see the Fisherman Bible Studyguide *Genesis 1–25: Walking with God.*

NOAH

Every "righteous man" in Scripture is a person of faith. Noah models the kind of faith
that shows itself in submission and obedience. The whole passage makes clear that
a Righteous God enforces righteousness
and without God's deliverance, no descen-
dant of Adam would escape the Creator's
judgment.

2

NOAH

GENESIS 6:5–7:24

Read Genesis 6:5–13.

1/What did God see when he looked at the earth?

2/In these verses what are the words and phrases which describe Noah?

Read Genesis 6:14–22.

3/What evidence do you find of God's affection and approval of Noah?

4/In order to walk with someone (rather than have them walk with you) what do you have to do?

5/Pretend you're Noah. In what ways would it have been hard to walk with God in the kind of world pictured in chapter six?

In what ways would it have been helpful to walk with God in that world?

Read Genesis 7.

6/What are the words and phrases in chapter seven which add to our picture of what Noah did to "walk with God"?

7/What would you have found especially hard about living on the ark?

8/Who benefitted by Noah's walk with God?

9/In what ways do other people benefit because you walk with God?

10/In the light of Noah's example, what can you do to walk with God? (Be specific.)

For further study on Noah, see the Fisherman Bible Studyguide *Genesis 1–25: Walking with God.*

ABRAHAM AND SARAH

In Abraham, God begins a covenant people who will bless the world—first with the
Law and ultimately with the Savior. Abraham and Sarah, like us, want to believe in
God's purpose for them but they have
some problems with how it works out in
the present.

3

ABRAHAM AND SARAH

GENESIS 12:1–13:4; 15:1–6; 16:1–6; 17:15–19; 18:1–15; 21:1–13; HEBREWS 11:8–19

Read Genesis 12:1–13:4.

1/What challenge and promise did God give to Abraham? (God later changed his name from Abram to Abraham and Sarai's to Sarah.) Why would God's words be a special challenge for Sarah at 65? (She was 10 years younger than her husband.)

2/What kind of priority did Abraham establish for himself and his household in Canaan (verses 7–8)? How was their faith tested (verse 10)?

3/What was motivating Abraham as he entered Egypt? Why? Read Genesis 20:8–13 where this situation was repeated with another king, Abimelech. (He and Sarah apparently agreed on the plan from the beginning.)

4/What were the consequences to Sarah, Abraham, and Pharaoh as a result of this plan? How did the Lord intervene for all of them?

Read Genesis 15:1–6; 16:1–6.

5/What suggestion did Sarah make to her husband? How cooperative was Abraham in the plan? What was missing in their discussion of her idea?

Note: In the Eastern culture of that time, if the master's wife was barren, a member of the household could be chosen to bear children for him. But just as in our day, what was culturally acceptable did not necessarily agree with God's will. God had promised offspring to Abraham through Sarah, and a monogamous marriage was his plan from the start (Gen. 2:24).

6/After Hagar became pregnant, what happened to Sarah's relationship with her? To Sarah's own sense of self-esteem? To Sarah's communication with her husband?

Read Genesis 17:15–19.

7/What special reassurance did God give to Sarah? (Sarah means "princess.") What do you think Abraham's laugh meant?

Read Genesis 18:1–15.

8/Why did Sarah laugh to herself at what she overheard? When do you think she realized who her guest was? What would it have taken for God's promise to be fulfilled?

Read Genesis 21:1–13.

9/How did God answer the question Sarah had asked in Genesis 18:13b? What was different about Sarah's laughter on this occasion? (Isaac means "laughter.")

Read Hebrews 11:8–19.

10/What attitudes enabled Abraham and Sarah to live by faith?

11/What does it mean to be an alien and a stranger on earth (verse 13)? How would a commitment to these roles affect your daily life?

For further study on Abraham and Sarah, see the Fisherman Bible Study-guide *Genesis 1–25: Walking with God.*

JOSEPH

Integrity amid impossible circumstances—that's the life story of Joseph. Why not give up, when nothing works out? This character makes clear that nothing is left to chance.

4

JOSEPH

GENESIS 39

Read Genesis 39.

1/Briefly explain how Joseph came to be in Potiphar's house. (If necessary, skim Genesis 37.)

2/What was Joseph's reputation in this Egyptian household? How did his responsibilities grow? Who was behind his success (verses 2–3)?

3/Why would the temptation to please Potiphar's wife be very strong?

ribe the qualities that mark Joseph's character? His
e?

ainst whom did Joseph refuse to sin? How was this a safeguard?

6/When trapped, how did Joseph handle sexual temptation? For New Testament instruction see 1 Corinthians 6:18. Then compare James 4:7. Why are we urged to *flee* in the one instance and *resist* in the other?

7/What sacrifice did Joseph make to preserve his personal integrity?

8/Considering Joseph's loneliness as a Jew in an Egyptian household, think of how easy it would have been to be involved in an indiscretion, especially since he was far from home. Are you using loneliness or misunderstanding as an excuse for sinning?

9/In light of Joseph's reputation, why would Potiphar assume his wife's story was accurate? Is there any evidence that he investigated its truth?

10/Imagine Joseph's feelings in prison. What new temptations would his injustice bring?

11/What made all the difference in Joseph's circumstances (verse 21)?

For further study on Joseph, see the Fisherman Bible Studyguide *Jacob and Joseph: Journeys toward God.*

MOSES

"I'd rather not get involved." That doesn't sound like the one who came down from Mount Sinai with the Ten Commandments. But that was his first reaction. And God persuaded him to get involved.

5

MOSES

EXODUS 3:1–4:17

Read Exodus 3:1–10.

1/Examine the scene Moses encountered in the desert. What emotions might have come to Moses in this desolate place? What might the passage convey by the mysterious phenomenon of the burning bush?

2/Many people find that geographically remote settings disorient them and make them feel detached from their roots or even from God. C. S. Lewis said he often felt spiritually weak when far from home in lonely hotel rooms. If this was Moses' feeling, how does this message from God reassure him? Does he seem to feel reassured?

3/In verse six, God links the present moment to the most famous ancestors of Moses. If you could select three or four famous people down through history, like Abraham, Isaac, and Jacob, which ones would make God's steadfast purpose seem most unshakeable to you?

Read Exodus 3:11-15.

4/Moses lodges a series of objections to the mission God has for him. There are two in this chapter and two in the next. Do you think the objection of verse 11 indicates modesty or cowardice? Does God's answer to him provide any immediate assurance?

5/Do you think self-confidence is determined by one's personality, circumstances, family upbringing, or something more? Are there clues in this passage to the confidence Moses had?

In verse 13, the objection anticipates a future problem Moses might have. The Israelites would ask about the "name" of God. This would be a question about God's revealed nature, since to the Semites the name disclosed the person. In verses 14-16 the name of God, a variation of *Yahweh,* the Covenant Keeping God, would be the permanent basis for the faith of God's pilgrim people. (Note: in most English Bibles, the small capital letters for LORD indicate the name *Yahweh* or *Jehovah.*)

6/How do verses 13-15 pull together past, present, and future in God's relationship to his people?

Read Exodus 3:16-22.

7/How does this scenario illustrate the faithful presence of the Lord that the earlier verses have implied?

8/The following are characteristics commonly displayed by God. See if this chapter documents them. (Group members can each take one and search through the passage.)

God's power

God's sovereign authority

God's knowledge of all things

God's permanence throughout history

God's purpose in history

God's special revelation to specific people

God's love and compassion

Read Exodus 4:1–9.

9/Moses' third objection raises a problem with implementing God's plan. Would this problem occur today?

10/The signs in verses 2–9 each confronted an Egyptian superstition: the snake was on Pharaoh's crown, leprosy was considered a curse, and the Nile River was regarded as almost divine. Moses would show that God's power triumphs easily over all human powers. Today you would have a different list of "sacred" superstitions and treasures. Name some examples in your circle of acquaintances.

11/Do you think Christians need evidence of God's reality today or is that a sign of weak faith?

Read Exodus 4:10–17.

12/Objection four! Was this speech issue a real problem or simply a baseless worry by Moses?

13/What is the link between our natural talents and the tasks God gives us? Does God match our mission to our talent?

14/If Moses were interviewed for the job of leading the Israelites out of Egypt, what would his strong and weak points be? Is he a "natural leader" at this point?

15/Think of the hardest thing you believe God wants you to do. Does your experience match Moses'? Which aspect of Moses' God will give you confidence to take the next step in your own mission?

DEBORAH

Deborah smashed the foes of Israel in battle and she still smashes stereotypes of Bible women. Who is this take-charge woman who rises in the moral chaos of the Judges?

6

DEBORAH

JUDGES 2:6-16, 18-19; 4:1-10; 5:1-31

Read Judges 2:6-16, 18-19 for background. Then read Judges 4:1-10.

1/At this time how formidable was Israel's enemy (verse 3)? For how long had Israel been dominated? From verses 4-5, describe Deborah's various roles. What kind of credibility had she established among the people?

2/Read Deuteronomy 16:18-20 for the qualifications of a judge. According to Judges 2:16 and 18, by whom had Deborah been appointed? What gave a judge confidence? Why would this be important?

3/What executive order did Deborah issue to Barak? By whose authority? Why was the military strategy significant? What guaranteed outcome did she declare (verse 7b)?

4/What did Barak's initial response (verse 8) reveal about his attitude to Deborah? How might his reluctance have affected the military conquest for the people as a whole (verse 7b)? For Barak personally (verse 9)? What gave Deborah her confidence?

5/After Barak marshalled his forces, what happened in the enemy camp? How might Barak have felt at that point? Discuss Deborah's challenge and Barak's response in verse 14.

6/How effective was Barak's counter attack (verse 16)? Why did Sisera feel safe with Jael? What did Jael accomplish and how did she do it?

7/Why is it significant that Barak was pursuing Sisera? What do you think went through Barak's mind when he saw Sisera?

8/How many of Deborah's predictions came true? How successful was her leadership?

Read Judges 5—The Song of Deborah.

This rousing song celebrates Israel's victory. It has been preserved not only as a record of historical events, but as a beautiful expression of praise to God. Deborah and Barak sang it as a duet.

9/What is it in leaders and all the people that brings praise to the Lord (verses 2, 9)? How did Deborah describe God (verses 4–5)? Herself (verse 7)? What added dimension does this title give to her character?

10/What character qualities do you admire most in Deborah? Though our culture and lifestyle are different today, in what specific ways should contemporary Christians follow her example?

For further study on Deborah, see the Fisherman Bible Studyguide *Women Who Achieved for God.*

RUTH

This ancestor of David and Jesus submitted to the circumstances of her life by submitting to the God of circumstances—a foreign God at first. She still models for us the transition from an outsider to an insider.

7

RUTH

RUTH 1:1–4:22

Read Ruth 1:1–5.

1/Describe the difficult circumstances of Naomi's stay in Moab.

Read Ruth 1:6–22.

2/What factors could have kept Ruth and Naomi apart? What was Ruth's response to Naomi's insistence that she return to her home?

3/Ruth's choice to go with Naomi is often seen as a type of "conversion." Why did Ruth's pledge mark a significant change in her life? How was that change similar to a person's decision to follow Christ?

Read Ruth 2:1–23.

4/What did Ruth's willingness to glean demonstrate about her character? What does the passage indicate about Ruth's attitude as she went out to glean?

5/When Ruth showed surprise at Boaz's consideration of her, he indicated that he had heard of her from the townspeople. What reputation had Ruth attained? How?

6/Boaz blessed Ruth because of "what she had done." According to Boaz, in whom had Ruth trusted? How had she demonstrated that trust? What actions had she taken that made her a recipient of his blessing?

7/Imagine Ruth and Naomi praying together after that first day's gleaning. Make a list of everything they had to thank God for.

Read Ruth 3:1-6.

8/Describe Naomi's plan for Ruth. Why was it important for Ruth to be vulnerable to Boaz? Why might this have been a difficult plan for Ruth to accept?

9/What was Ruth's reply to Naomi? What does this demonstrate about the relationship between Ruth and Naomi?

Read Ruth 3:7-18.

10/What was Boaz's response to Ruth? What did his blessing in verse 10 demonstrate about Ruth's priorities—and about her obedience to God?

11/Review Naomi's prayer for Ruth in Ruth 1:8-9 and Boaz's prayer for Ruth in 2:12. In what ways was God beginning to answer those prayers?

Read Ruth 4:1–22.

12/Both Ruth and Boaz are called by name in Matthew's genealogy of Jesus Christ. How is the presence of Ruth (a non-Israelite) in the lineage of Christ (Matthew 1:5) an indication of (a) his purposes in coming to earth; and (b) the plan of salvation?

13/Ruth 4:14 (NIV) reads: "Praise be to the Lord, who this day has not left you without a kinsman-redeemer." In light of the offspring of Ruth and Boaz, how was this an appropriate blessing?

14/Ruth's life demonstrates the principles of faithfulness, humility, obedience, and fruitfulness. How can your life, in your present situation, reflect these same godly characteristics?

For further study on Ruth, see the Fisherman Bible Studyguides *Ruth and Daniel: God's People in an Alien Society, Friendship: Portraits in God's Family Album,* and *Women Who Believed God.*

DAVID

Of all the Old Testament characters in this book, David has one of the most distinct personalities. His psalms we know well and the episodes of his life are familiar. Here is someone like ourselves—emotionally and spiritually. And his resources are comparable to our own.

8

DAVID

2 SAMUEL 11:1–12:14; PSALM 32

Read 2 Samuel 11:1–5.

1/According to verse 1, where should David have been? How do David's actions (verse 2) indicate a lack of anything constructive to do?

2/What phrases in verses 2–4 show the progression of David's lust? How were David's emotion, mind, and will involved? What was the first consequence of David's sin?

Read 2 Samuel 11:6–27.

3/What steps did David take in attempting to cover up his sin?

4/How did David respond to Joab's message? How was rationalizing Uriah's death a comfort to David?

5/Why does one sin often lead to another? What evidence of sin's entrapment have you observed? How can an understanding of sin's nature help you resist temptation?

Secure in his cover-up, David married Bathsheba and went about conducting the affairs of state. Nearly one year passed between the end of chapter 11 and the beginning of chapter 12.

Read 2 Samuel 12:1–14.

6/How was the parable of the poor man's lamb appropriate for showing David his sin? Why was David's response so strong? How did his reaction to the story set him up for Nathan's rebuke?

7/List the things that God had done and would do for David (see verses 7 and 8). What was the root of David's sin? How did God's two judgments correspond to David's sins of adultery and murder?

8/Characterize the tone and content of David's reply to God's judgment. What other emotions was David probably feeling that are not recorded here? Why was his simple reply the best response (see 1 John 1:9)?

Read Psalm 32.

9/How does David describe the person who is blessed (verses 1–2)?

10/This psalm was written by David as a part of his struggle with God after the sins recorded in 2 Samuel 11. What did unconfessed sin do in David's life (verses 3–4)?

11/What happened when David acknowledged his sin?

12/Identify the advice and the promises given to the godly in verses 6–10.

13/How does David express his renewed relationship with God (verse 11)? What have been the results of confession and trusting in your life? Can you shout for joy right now? Why or why not?

For further study on David, see the Fisherman Bible Studyguides *Relationships* and *David: Man after God's Own Heart, Volumes I and II.*

ELIJAH

Ever wish God would just speak up and show his preferences? On occasion he has made his feelings clear. Elijah was satisfied—for a time.

9

ELIJAH

1 KINGS 18; 19:1–18

Read 1 Kings 18:1–19.

1/Why did Elijah return to Israel? Briefly suggest reasons for Jezebel's attack on the Lord's prophets (verse 4) and for Ahab's frantic search for Elijah (verse 10). See 1 Kings 17:1.

2/Describe Elijah's attitude as he confronted King Ahab. What was the source of his security?

Read 1 Kings 18:20–29.

3/Describe Elijah's confrontation with the people on Mt. Carmel. How did the prophet summarize the nation's spiritual dilemma? Why did the people have no answer for Elijah? Considering the circumstances of the previous three-and-a-half years, what do you think the people thought of him, and why?

4/Summarize the contest "rules," and how the "winner" was to be determined.

5/Describe the efforts of the prophets of Baal to get their god to answer their prayers. How does Scripture emphasize the futility of their efforts? Specifically, *why* was there no answer? In your own words summarize Elijah's mocking rebuke (verse 27).

Read 1 Kings 18:30–40.

6/After carefully fulfilling the levitical law in the preparation of the bull offering for sin, what did Elijah ask the people to do? Why? Considering the extent of the drought, what did the pouring out of their scarce water (probably brought along on the journey to Carmel) require of the people?

7/How did Elijah address the Lord in his prayer? Why? What specific petitions did he make?

8/How did God answer? Describe the reaction of the people. How would the death of the Baal prophets by the hands of the people help restore their faith and obedience?

Read 1 Kings 18:41–46.

9/What was Elijah's advice to Ahab (verse 41)? How did Elijah describe his expectation of the rain? What does this description show about Elijah's faith?

10/How do you think Elijah's servant felt as he reported six times, "There is nothing"? What might his wording of the seventh report indicate about his faith? What was Elijah's response to the seventh report?

Read 1 Kings 19:1–18.

11/Having just experienced the extraordinary power of God on Mt. Carmel and the successful siege of prayer for rain, what do you think Elijah anticipated as he sped toward Jezreel, the headquarters of Jezebel and the nation's center of Baal worship?

52

12/Summarize how Jezebel received the news of the events on Mt. Carmel. What was Elijah's reaction to Jezebel's threat? What specific instruction was missing as Elijah began this journey? (See 1 Kings 17:2,8; 18:1,46.)

13/How did Elijah's desire in verse 4 contradict the very reason he ran away? Briefly summarize God's treatment of his fearful and fatigued prophet. What did God do? What did he not do?

14/What did God ask Elijah to do? What was he teaching Elijah by refusing to show himself in exciting displays of nature's power? Why was this an important lesson for the prophet to learn at this particular time?

15/Summarize God's remedy for Elijah's depression and self-righteous retirement (verses 15–16). What effect might Elisha's appointment have had on him? What effects might his learning about the seven thousand faithful people have had on him? How has God encouraged you in the low times of your life?

For further study on Elijah, see the Fisherman Bible Studyguide *Elijah: Obedience in a Threatening World.*

DANIEL

Here is a Bible character who, unlike many
of the others, had to live in a hostile culture
that made no pretense of serving the Revealed God of Israel. In this way he closely
parallels the modern Christian. All who
have ever felt conspicuous because of a
conviction will find Daniel a fellow pilgrim.

10

DANIEL

DANIEL 1:1–21; 2:27–49; 4:19–37; 5:5–30

Read Daniel 1:1–21.

1/Why was Daniel initially taken into King Nebuchadnezzar's court?

2/How are Daniel and the other young Israelites described (verse 4)?

3/How were Daniel and his friends equipped to fulfill the king's expectations of them (verse 17)?

4/Why did Daniel refuse the rich foods and wines provided by the king? How did he obtain official permission to maintain his conviction?

5/Why was it important for Daniel to obtain permission not to eat the king's food? Why did he not simply refuse it or dispose of it without the officer's knowledge?

6/How did God honor Daniel's commitment to personal purity?

Read Daniel 2:27–49; 4:19–37; 5:5–30.

7/When Daniel interpreted Nebuchadnezzar's first dream (2:27–48), the interpretation was a favorable one. How did Daniel demonstrate his personal integrity in the interpretation of Nebuchadnezzar's second dream (4:19–37)?

8/What risks did Daniel take in offering the second interpretation?

9/Nebuchadnezzar's son Belshazzar called for Daniel to interpret the "hand-writing on the wall" (5:5–30). What details show that Daniel gave an honest and accurate evaluation of the message? What risks were inherent in this interpretation?

10/What did his refusal to accept Belshazzar's gifts (5:17) reveal about Daniel's personal character?

11/Both in his personal practices and in his interaction with foreign kings, what principles did Daniel adhere to? What do they demonstrate about Daniel's character? About his relationship to God?

12/Although most twentieth-century Christians don't live in exile or under service to foreign powers, they often face circumstances that challenge their personal beliefs and actions. What circumstances do you face in daily life that challenge your faith? Have you had any recent successes (or failures) of personal integrity when you have been tempted to compromise? How can Daniel's example of integrity be an encouragement to you?

For further study on Daniel, see the Fisherman Bible Studyguide *Ruth and Daniel: God's People in an Alien Society*.

ELIZABETH

Like Noah, Abraham, Sarah, and Moses, this figure shows that old age is not a time to give up on spiritual growth. We never know when God has something else for us to do.

11

ELIZABETH

LUKE 1:5–25, 36–37, 39–45, 56–66, 80

Read Luke 1:5–25.

1/What common heritage did Elizabeth share with her husband? From verses 5–7 how would you describe Elizabeth's character? Her problems? Her way of life? Her spiritual commitment?

2/Describe in your own words the setting for Gabriel's appearance. Compare the angel's words with the prophecy made about 400 years earlier in Malachi 4:5–6.

3/How did Zechariah react to the angel's announcement? Why?

60

4/How did Zechariah communicate to the people? What did Elizabeth's reaction to these unexpected events reveal about her?

5/If you had been in her place and received the tremendous honor of bearing the special messenger of Jesus Christ, would you have broadcast the news or kept quiet? Why or why not?

Read Luke 1:36-37, 39-45, 56.

6/What did Elizabeth's reception of a pregnant unmarried teenager reveal about Elizabeth's character? How did Elizabeth apparently feel about a much younger woman having been given the greater honor? (See verses 42-43.)

7/In what specific ways did Elizabeth support and encourage Mary? For how long? What did she emphasize in verse 45?

Read Luke 1:57–66, 80.

8/What did John's birth reveal about Elizabeth's relationship with her family and neighbors? From verses 13 and 59–63, what can you gather about her communication with her husband? What kind of reaction did this event, including Elizabeth and Zechariah's relationship with each other, have on the community?

9/How is John's development described (verse 80)? Read John the Baptist's description of his own ministry in John 3:28–30. How did his attitude reflect that of his mother's in Luke 1:42–43?

10/From what you have read about Elizabeth, what do you think helped her to build such positive relationships with her family? With her community? With people who were in trouble?

11/How do Hebrews 11:6 and Psalm 37:3–4 apply to Elizabeth? In what ways can you strengthen your family relationship? How can you use your home to encourage others, especially those in trouble?

For further study on Elizabeth, see the Fisherman Bible Studyguide *Friendship: Portraits in God's Family Album.*

MARY

After years of Christmas plays and stories, who of us can turn to Scripture alone and study the mother of Jesus in a fresh light? Here is a sister in faith, one who had derived the best from Israel's religion and revelation. And her life, like ours, joined crisis and Christ.

12

MARY

LUKE 1:26–40, 46–56

Read Luke 1:26–40, 46–56.

1/What did Gabriel say about Mary's relationship with God (verses 28, 30)?

2/Why did the announcement trouble Mary? What did this reveal about her character?

3/How did Gabriel describe her future child?

4/Why would the news about Elizabeth have been an encouragement to Mary?

5/How was Mary's response in verse 38 an act of worship? What attitude toward God did her response indicate?

6/Following Gabriel's dramatic announcement Mary went to her cousin Elizabeth's home. What did Elizabeth recognize about Mary's relationship with God?

7/Verses 46–55 contain Mary's song of praise, commonly called the Magnificat. What do these verses reveal about her relationship with God?

8/Write down every term or phrase she used to describe God in her worship. How would you describe her concept of God? What did she know about him?

9/What had Mary learned about God from history? Compare her expressions of praise with these statements from the Old Testament: Psalm 103:17, Isaiah 40:22–24, Job 5:11–12, Psalm 107:9. How do you think Mary knew all these great truths about God? See Deuteronomy 6:4–7.

10/What characteristic of Mary's is shown in Luke 2:19, 51–52? What did she do after Jesus' ascension? (See Acts 1:12–14).

11/Why is our concept of God important to true worship? How can we grow in our knowledge of God? How can Mary's life encourage you in your walk with God?

For further study on Mary, see the Fisherman Bible Studyguide *Friendship: Portraits in God's Family Album*.

PETER

Extroverts can get themselves into trouble: they talk too much and jump to conclusions. But most people feel comfortable around them. Peter leads, but sometimes leads astray; he feels, but sometimes lets his feelings run away with reality. In the end he found his personality changing under the power of the Spirit.

13
PETER

MATTHEW 4:18-20; JOHN 21:1-19; ACTS 4:8-13

Read Matthew 4:18-20.

1/For what purpose did Jesus call Peter (verse 19)? What does this mean?

2/When Peter followed Jesus, what did he leave behind (verse 20)? If you have responded to Jesus' call, what have you left behind?

Read John 21:1-14.

These events occurred after Jesus' death and resurrection.

3/What do you learn about Peter from these verses? How could the Lord use Peter's character traits for his purpose of making Peter a fisher of men?

4/What distinctive character traits has God created in you? Think of a few specific ways that he might use these for his purposes.

Read John 21:15–19.

5/Three times Jesus repeats another purpose he has for Peter's life. What is it? How is this purpose linked to Jesus' original call to Peter?

6/What does Jesus' commission indicate about his confidence in Peter's future ministry?

7/What more does Jesus tell Peter in this passage? What purpose will Peter's death serve?

Note: Ancient writers state that about thirty-four years after this, Peter was crucified, and that he begged to be crucified with his head downwards, not considering himself worthy to die in the same posture in which his Lord did.

Read Acts 4:8–13.

8/What astonished the leaders about Peter and John (verse 13)? Of what did they take note (verse 13)?

9/In what ways was Peter fulfilling God's purpose for him?

For further study on Peter, see the Fisherman Bible Studyguide *Relationships* and *Acts: 1–12: God Moves in the Early Church.*

PAUL

More than any other writer in our Bible, Paul's writings have shaped our church life, theology, and missionary emphasis. Through him we understand the gospel of grace in which Christ's work fully meets our spiritual poverty. This study takes us to the starting line.

14

PAUL

ACTS 7:54–8:3; 9:1–31

We first meet Saul (whose name was later changed to Paul) in Acts 7, as he witnesses the death of Stephen by stoning. (Stephen was a leader in the early church.)

Read Acts 7:54–8:3.

1/What effect did Stephen's death seem to have on Saul?

Read Acts 9:1–19a.

2/What was still Saul's purpose (9:1–2)? Read Acts 26:9–11 for Paul's own statement about the intensity of his opposition to Christians.

3/In what dramatic way did God get Saul's attention? In harassing the Christians, who had Saul really been persecuting? What did Jesus tell Saul to do?

4/How did this encounter affect Saul physically? How did it affect his traveling companions? Why do you think Jesus chose to meet Saul in such a dramatic way?

5/What words would you use to describe Ananias? What job did the Lord assign him? Why did he hesitate? What reassured him? How did his obedience demonstrate his faith?

6/What did the Lord reveal about Saul's destiny? What was Saul's attitude as he waited to hear from God? In your own words, describe what happened to him when he met Ananias.

Note: In Galatians 1:15–18 we learn that Saul spent 3 years in Arabia. Exactly when Saul left for Arabia is not clear. However, shortly after his conversion he went away to spend time alone with God.

Read Acts 9:19b–31.

7/Contrast Saul in verse 1 with Saul in verses 20–22, 27. Why would preaching in the synagogue demand courage? How did Saul identify Jesus to the people?

8/How disturbing was Saul's preaching to the Jews (verses 23–24, 29)? How was the Lord's prediction of verse 16 beginning to be fulfilled? Why do you think God's purposes for Saul included suffering?

9/Why were the Jerusalem believers hesitant to accept Saul? Suppose your father or son had been one of those previously seized by Saul, imprisoned, and perhaps put to death. How would you feel if he wanted to join your fellowship of Christians? What would you suspect?

10/Who bridged the gap? Read Acts 4:36. How was Barnabas living out the meaning of his name?

11/Read the summary statement made about the church in verse 31. How successful had its enemies been in stamping out Christianity? How is the story of Saul and the church an encouragement to Christians today who are persecuted for their faith?

For further study on Paul, see the Fisherman Bible Studyguide *Paul: 13th Apostle* and *Relationships*.

BARNABAS

At last—"ordinary people." But Barnabas was extraordinary in his own way. And when you need a Barnabas, no Paul, Peter, or Moses will do.

15

BARNABAS

ACTS 4:32–37; 9:19b–28; 11:19-30; 13:1–13, 42–52; 14:1–28; 15

Read Acts 4:32–37.

1/Who was Barnabas? What was his background? What was his probable social standing?

Read Acts 9:19b–28.

2/How influential was Barnabas in the church of Jerusalem? How do you know? Put yourself in Saul's (Paul's) place. What would Barnabas' help have meant to you?

Read Acts 11:19–30.

3/Describe Barnabas' ministry in Antioch. What seems to have been his chief gift? What was the significance of Barnabas going to Tarsus to look for Saul? Humanly speaking, who was responsible for Saul's involvement in this church?

4/Take five minutes (or longer, if needed) to evaluate yourself as an encourager. Ask God to show you who in your circle of relationships needs building up. Make a list of these people, then make a commitment to be their encourager this week, either in person, or by phone or letter.

Skim Acts 13:1-13, 42-52; 14:1-28.

5/Note that Saul's name was changed to Paul in Acts 13:9. Who sent Barnabas and Paul on their first missionary journey? Why do you think they were chosen?

6/Who quickly emerged as the chief spokesman? (Support your answer by giving references. Note the change in order in 13:2 and 13:46).

Skim Acts 15.

7/What do you see of Barnabas' influence and encouragement in both the journey to Jerusalem (verse 3) and at the council in Jerusalem? Why was it crucial that Barnabas and Paul be at the meeting (verse 12)? What was their role after the council meeting (verse 22, 25, 35)?

8/What contention later arose between Paul and Barnabas (verses 36–41)? (John Mark's family background is recorded in Colossians 4:10 and Acts 12:12.) How did the solution to the disagreement fit in with what we have come to expect of Barnabas?

9/How did Paul describe Mark in Philemon 24? Read 2 Timothy 4:6 and 11. How would you describe Paul's final relationship to Mark as he wrote his last letter just before he died?

10/What price did Barnabas pay to stick with John Mark?

11/Share briefly from your own experience how someone believed in you and helped you learn and change.

For further study on Barnabas, see the Fisherman Bible Studyguide *Friend-ship: Portraits in God's Family Album.*

PRAYER NOTEBOOK

date	request	date of answer

date	request	date of answer

FISHERMAN BIBLE STUDYGUIDES

Check your local bookstore or write **Harold Shaw Publishers, Box 567, Wheaton, Illinois**